To: CASSANDRA
A very special woman of God
God IS proud of you!!

Larry Williams

Watchman of Souls

Larry Williams

authorHOUSE®

AuthorHouse™
1663 Liberty Drive
Bloomington, IN 47403
www.authorhouse.com
Phone: 1-800-839-8640

© 2011 Larry Williams. All rights reserved.

No part of this book may be reproduced, stored in a retrieval system, or transmitted by any means without the written permission of the author.

First published by AuthorHouse   3/11/2011

ISBN: 978-1-4567-4812-8 (sc)
ISBN: 978-1-4567-4807-4 (e)
ISBN: 978-1-4567-4811-1 (hc)

Library of Congress Control Number: 2011903025

Printed in the United States of America

Any people depicted in stock imagery provided by Thinkstock are models, and such images are being used for illustrative purposes only. Certain stock imagery © Thinkstock.

This book is printed on acid-free paper.

Because of the dynamic nature of the Internet, any Web addresses or links contained in this book may have changed since publication and may no longer be valid. The views expressed in this work are solely those of the author and do not necessarily reflect the views of the publisher, and the publisher hereby disclaims any responsibility for them.

Introduction

You shall know the truth
And the truth shall make you free
John 8:32 is necessary
If you truly want to see

Someone asked Jesus
Will only a few go to Heaven because of sin
Jesus said the road to Heaven is straight and narrow
You must practice holy living if you want to get in

I thank God for this opportunity
His truth has made me free
We all have our own ministries
And this is how he deals with me

About The Author

Larry Williams is a native of Garland, Arkansas by way of Texarkana, Arkansas. He does not claim any special accolades or boast of numerous credentials. He is simply a willing vessel being used by God. Larry is a man who has a passion for righteousness and a heart of compassion for all people. God has given him the ability to minister his word in the form of poetry, the message that he carries is challenging, encouraging, enlightening and unexpected. His goal is to see souls saved all over the world and this is his assignment at this point and time in his life. He believes that it is when we are challenged that we can reach our full potential.

About The Book

There has been a conviction placed on my heart for many years to write this book of inspirational poems and words of encouragement for God's people. It has led me to write of many personal conflicts, fears and problems that plague God's people today as well as words of encouragement and praise and thanksgiving that so often beset our trials and tribulations. It is not my intention to offend or judge anyone who is reading this book, I stand first in line to say that I'm not perfect and that I fall from time to time too but God has a mandate on my life and every other Christian to live a Holy life style. I only wrote as the spirit of God was laid on my heart to do so, I pray that this book will bring enlightenment, courage and strength of heart to any who may read these words as it has my own and be a blessing to all people.

A Watchman Of Souls

A watchman of souls
God Anointed and said take a stand
There's no choice in this matter
Or the blood of souls will be left in his hands

A spirit filled with love
Love that corrects to make one whole
Priceless is its value
A righteous message not a form of control

Turn from your wicked ways
Is the message that has been placed in his ear
The highway to Heaven is straight and narrow
And that is the message that people must hear

God says live Holy
Don't let the truth go untold
I'm just the messenger
A watchman of souls

Larry Williams

Come As You Are

Come as you are
Even if you just look plain
But sometimes people get frowned upon
Because tradition doesn't say the same

Come as you are
Regardless of the color of your skin
Racial prejudice doesn't have a place in Christ
It's not of God and it's a sin

Come as you are
Descent is all that's required, when it comes to your clothes
God wants to see you fixed up on the inside
The church's concern should be your soul

Satan Says

Nothing unrighteous moves me
I sit around these churches week after week
The power of God is missing
I can tell when they pray and they speak
I'm an evil spirit
It takes righteousness to outdo me
Most of you won't live like this
And I don't have to flee
Most churches today
Only have a form of Godliness
It's not the real thing
I love going to these places
I like to buck, shout and scream
The choir sounds really good
That was my job and I did it well
I hope none of them are saved
We can sing and live together in hell
Oh yeah' the apple of my eye
A hypocriting preacher, what a dream
Causing souls to stay unsaved and lost
That's the reason why I sing
What joy comes to my heart
When I see you, using my schemes
Fighting cussin and fussin
Acting wicked and being mean
Just wanted you to know that I'm here
And if you need me don't bother to call
I'll be the one back stabbing, cutting your throat
And waiting for you to fall

A Choice

What a joy life can be
Being free and on the go
This world has a lot to offer
And this we all know

But did you know, that there is a king named Jesus
Who sits high upon a throne
Looking down on all the world
Noticing the seeds that we have sown

His father is the creator of all things
That includes you and me
He designed us in his image
And that's how he wants us to be

But then he gives a choice
He won't twist your arm to make you pray
He says choose this day whom you'll serve
And we'll resolve the issue on judgment day

A Good Man

A good man is reasonable
But firm when he speaks
And just because he respects you
Doesn't mean he's weak

A good man stands his ground
When he knows that he's not wrong
Some say he's just crazy
And leaves him standing all alone

A good man fears the Lord
And he knows where to stand
God has ordered his steps
And that's why he's a good man

A Good Woman

A good woman is the key
To the heart of a man
She can unlock his potential
Like no other can

She is a wise and loving woman
Considers God when it's time to choose
But don't take her kindness for weakness
Or you will be the one to loose

Her beauty comes from within
She is strong when the days are hard
Her goodness is divinely directed
Because it comes from the Lord

A Mother's Love

A mother's love is unique
Like no other you can find
It looks over our mistakes
And gives a word that is kind

A mother's love is from God
A gift beyond compare
It truly is a blessing
And something we can share

A mother's love is a treasure
Worth more than diamonds and pearls
Thank God that it exist
We need it in this world

A Relationship With God

A relationship with God
Is what makes your life complete
It makes you a peaceful person
Especially when you speak

Knowing that he's your source
Will fill your heart with joy
Satan won't be able to defeat you
And play with you as a toy

A relationship with God
Will cast away your fears
You will know that He has all power
And there is no need for tears

Gain your relationship
And treasure it with your heart
Let the love of God flow freely
From you to others, this is your part

A Sinner's Prayer

Good morning Lord
Yes it's me again
Sorry for my tardiness
Last night was a full night of sin
I drank good whisky and wine
Even had a shot of gin
Some people looked at me shamefully
But my pastor said that I have been born again
He said I'll make mistakes
But you provide mercy and grace
He told me to pay my tithes and give a love offering
And in Heaven I would have a place
I feel really blessed
That you and my pastor are so close
He said that my sins are covered
And tells me what I like the most
But there is one thing on my mind
And Lord I'm not joking
Something on the inside of me
Says I'm going to bust Hell wide open

A Sinner's Prayer Answered

God answered the sinner's prayer
And He answered him in his dreams
He said I'm Holy and my word stands forever
And that's exactly what I mean

People lie on me for money
And in my son's name
But I am the Lord of Lords and king of kings
And son" I don't play games

I know that your heart is pure
And that you have been used and led astray
But you are my "little child"
And I dare anyone to treat you that way

Don't stop going to church
I said to assemble and I made it plain
Live your life Holy because I am watching you
And always pray in my son's name

A Watchman Of Souls

A watchman of souls
God Anointed and said take a stand
There's no choice in this matter
Or the blood of souls will be left in his hands

A spirit filled with love
Love that corrects to make one whole
Priceless is its value
A righteous message not a form of control

Turn from your wicked ways
Is the message that has been placed in his ear
The highway to Heaven is straight and narrow
And that is the message that people must hear

God says live Holy
Don't let the truth go untold
I'm just the messenger
A watchman of souls

All I Can Do

Lord I've done
All I can do
My spirit is now weary
I'm leaving the rest up to you

I've done my best
According to your word
I have sent prayers out
Praying that they would be heard

Lord will your word
Fall upon deaf ears
I pray that it doesn't
The result will be tears

Lord I have done
All I can do
I can't be heard
So I give this thing to you

Another Number

Are you just another number
Another face in the crowd
Or are you God's remnant
One whom He can trust and be proud

Don't be just another number
To be counted at the door
For God has a purpose for you
It's what you were made for

Regardless of your number
Or where you fall in line
Remember the most important thing
Is to have a Godly mind

Stand up to be counted
If being present releases your fear
Numbers don't mean much to God
It's how you live your life while you are here

Are you Ready

God tells me to just tell it like it is
The truth is what sets us free
Blood stained hands will never reach Heaven
So the truth is what you will get from me

First of all are you ready
If you die today, who will be keeper of your eternal soul
No one is guaranteed tomorrow
And everybody won't live to get old

I know tradition says you are saved forever
Jesus paid it all and your salvation is securely locked in
But mounds of hot coals will be burning at your feet
If you don't turn your back to willful sin

Everybody is not going to Heaven
So I won't overwhelm you with lies
Judgment day is fast approaching
It's better to know where you are going than to be surprised

Awake

Awake oh you sleepers
The wool has been pulled over your eyes
Darkness has over taken you
Satan has convinced you with his lies

He told you that it's okay
To embrace the world because it needs a friend
He said back sliding has never hurt anyone
So will you be having vodka or a shot of gin

Just a little leverage
Is all he needs and he will pull you in
He will kill your witness with just one blow
And cover you with a cloth of sin

Awaken sleeping saint
The world has an eye on you
But more important than that
God is watching too

Backslider

Backslider
It's time for you to choose
God is not mocked
You either win with Him or you lose

I know you've been told
That grace will get you in
But God says live Holy
And give up your life of sin

Don't be found
Out of God's will
Satan's on the hunt
For your soul to steal

Be Careful Whom You Pray To

Be careful whom you pray to
In these last days
Your prayers are directed
To the God that you Praise

The God you serve
Is the God you Pray to
Check the fruit of the spirit
Decide what you should do

Knowing who your God is
Is the best choice
God Almighty says
"That his sheep shall know his voice"

So be careful whom you pray to
For Satan has an ear
All those who follow Him
Their prayers he will hear

Larry Williams

Be The Servant

God said be the servant
And help those in need
Make a way for someone else
It will be a Godly deed

To truly be a servant
It starts in your Heart
The work that is done
Is not written on a chart

Serve out of love
For it's the only way
To truly be God's servant
This is your price to pay

Become a Mirror

Sometimes love ones and others
Can really rub us the wrong way
Seems that logic has taken the back seat
And the brain is out to play

Become a mirror for these people
So they can see what's being done wrong
It's easy to give out but hard to receive
The resolution shouldn't be long

Bible On The Shelf

Is your Bible on the shelf
Do you know what it's worth
If you look at it closely
It's the basic instructions before leaving Earth

The Bible is the manual
For your mind body and soul
If it's left on the shelf
How can you be made whole

The Bible is life
It is alive and well
To lie dusty on a shelf
Could cause a soul to see hell

Born Again

For it is written
Jesus said ye must be born again
If we want to enter heaven
This is the only way to get in

Just going to church won't do
Your spirit has to be born again
This transformation is spiritual
Within The heart is where it begins

Old things are passed away
And all has become new
God's love will take over
Regardless of what people do

So go to God
And turn your back to sin
Claim Jesus as your savior
And you will be born again

Except a man be born again
He cannot see the kingdom of God (John) 3:3

But God I Went To Church

But God, I went to church
And I paid my tithes
But you also gambled with your salvation
And told many lies

I even sang in the choir
And opened up the church
Did you refuse Satan's temptations
And tell Him, that I was first

That alcohol I drank
I just wanted a sample
Did you know that people were watching
And you were setting a bad example

But I always went to church
I talked about it boldly
But did you know me in spirit
And live your Holy

Church Hoppers

Church Hoppers have gotten quiet popular
They are known all over town
Looking and searching for fulfillment in God
Where ever it can be found

This is such an ugly name for saints
And it's all because somebody got mad
Mad because people left their church
And all in the name of Jesus, this is really sad

Now just getting down to facts
These so called church hoppers are really scattered sheep
The shepherds are calling them goats and laughing
But God is watching and I would find it hard to sleep

Come As You Are

Come as you are
Even if you just look plain
But sometimes people get frowned upon
Because tradition doesn't say the same

Come as you are
Regardless of the color of your skin
Racial prejudice doesn't have a place in Christ
It's not of God and it's a sin

Come as you are
Descent is all that's required, when it comes to your clothes
God wants to see you fixed up on the inside
The church's concern should be your soul

Compliments

Don't be caught up
By the compliments of men
Keep your focus on God
And your life free from sin

Let God's word
Be the judge of your life
And you will be the one
To discern what is right

We can think we're at our best
Boast, talk loud and brag
But in the eyesight of God
We are yet as filthy rags

Do You Know What Time It Is

It is time
For the truth to be told
If you die without God
You're sure to lose your soul

It's time to show God
That we're faithful and true
We're not playing games
That's not what saints do

It's time to stand for Jesus
And cast out demons in HIS name
But if we live as hypocrites
The demons will remain

It's time to bless God
And turn our lives around
Let's go evangelize the world
And tell them what we've found

Doers Of The Word

Doers of the word
With you God is well pleased
You know your purpose in life
And he is your only need

Continue to be a doer
And do not turn away
For you have a seat in Heaven
This is safe to say

Doers of the Word
Your day will soon come
The persecution will cease
And your work will be done

Drama Lovers

Drama lovers come in all different sizes
And in all colors of faces
They will show up all at once
And in some of the most unexpected places

Drama is their number one concern
They love to argue and don't try to reason or understand
Most of the time there isn't a problem
They create drama because they can

A drama lover is always right
They will take time out, to explain to you what you did wrong
So the next time this person shows up
Start praying for the spirit of peace and watch them leave you alone

Dry Your Eye

Dry your eye
And cry no more
The Lord's in charge
He'll settle the score

Learn to rejoice
When the clouds hang low
God wants to see Faith
Let yours show

So dry your eye
And find peace in the word
Your mountain will move
You'll be as free as the birds

Faith

We claim we have Faith
But yet we fail test
Our faith is in denial
And we find it hard to rest

Deny yourself
It's not about you
We're here as Servants
With God's work to do
What do you want
What is it that you're needing
Jesus paid the price on the cross
With his blood suffering and bleeding

What more can you ask for
It's already been done
We should be sealed in Faith
Our Battle has already been won

Go Back To God

My sister and my brother
Please lend me your ear
God has delivered a message to me
One that you simply must hear

Hypocrites are in the midst
Of many churches using His name
Lots of traditions have been applied
But God never said the same

Don't let man mislead you
With his ungodly deeds
Our God is the God of all that is Holy
He's the one who supplies our needs

Many of you have left church
Pointing fingers and looking back
You have to answer to God for your self
Do you think he will be pleased with that

Go back to God
He will deal with all that is unclean
The book of life has daily entries
You won't have to say a thing

God Is Speaking

Why would you call me Lord, Lord
And do not the things that I say
Your actions would be as a hypocrite
It is in your best interest to change your ways today

Tomorrow is promised to no one
There has been plenty of time
I gave my son for your life
And vengeance will be mine

For I am a Holy God
And holy my people shall be
Don't go on deceiving yourselves
If it's my kingdom you plan to see

God's Marriage

May the peace of God
Rest upon your souls
As your spiritual union
And lives are made whole

To God be the glory
For this marriage today
This couple made sure
That God paved the way

They both know God
And plan to serve
As a couple
According to His word

To be in God
Is to be in love
This marriage is Holy sanctified
And directed from above

God's Prosperity

Do you want to prosper
And have good success
Then keep God's law
And He will do the rest

Don't let people rob you
Saying give, give, give
Get to know God's word
And you will know how to live

God is the way
Not money and things
Be a good steward over what you have
And you can reach your dreams

The word says seek first God's kingdom and righteousness
And the rest shall come
If you truly believe
Let His will be done

Happy Birthday Jesus

God gave his son Jesus
To die for our sins
Let's stop playing around
It's time to make amends

It's time to repent
For all we've done wrong
Today is the day
To learn a new song

Happy Birthday Jesus
Would be a good title
But you would still have some
To sit there arrogant and idle

So no more excuses
And no more delays
It's time to serve God truly
In all our ways

God is not mocked
You will reap' what you sow
Christmas is Jesus' birthday
Just make sure that you know

Heaven Knows

The door is securely locked
The window blinds are closed
But God's eye is open
And Heaven certainly knows

There is nothing you can hide
Don't fool yourself
Judgment Day is near
Get right or get left

Hold On

In the time of opposition
What will you do
Your response will show all
How the spirit operates in you

So hold on
To God's unchanging hand
It's in your faith
Whether you fall or stand

Be of good cheer
And do not faint
Keep praising God
That's a real saint

Just count it all joy
When the storm blows in
Show the world that you're anchored
And you've turned your back to sin

Holy

God says that He is Holy
And His people shall be as well
Holy is the path that leads to Heaven
All other roads are short cuts to hell

Holiness is not a denomination
God says this is how we should live
Pure at heart and righteous
Unselfish and ready to give

Jesus died for our sins
God really loves us well
Remember the Lord is not mocked
If you're Holy time will tell

Old things are passed away
And all has become new
Let's shake our tree of life
And see what fruit falls through

Holy is the Lamb of God
Nothing else will do
Let's pray that blinded eyes will open
To live Holy is up to you

Husband And Wife

Husband and Wife
Are meant to be together for life
Put God first
And your marriage will be nice

Show love to one another
All your days through
Satan will be ashamed
He won't know what to do

Satan will surely use
Any willing vessel
Keep him out of your lives
God made marriage, it's special

I Am Tradition

I am tradition
And religion is my best friend
We have our own set of rules
So you'll just have to fit in

Personally, I don't like surprises
That Holy Spirit and me, we don't get alone
He changes the order of service too much
I do things all on my own

I like things done a certain way
And by one that I appointed
That Holy Spirit is just so different
He calls on those who are anointed

Where the spirit of the Lord is
The people are set free
But I am tradition
And you will never be free with me

No yokes are broken
No one is ever healed
Something is just not adding up
Because the spirit of God is real

I Found Out

I found out
That this world is not my home
And once I stop breathing
My soul will be gone

There's nothing I can do
Or nothing I can say
If I don't choose God
And live His way

I found out
That I have to live right
And put down my fist
This is a spiritual fight

I Got Saved

I got saved friend
I'm no longer the same
My heart is filled with love
It's such a wonderful change

I've gone to church for years
Thinking that I must be okay
But God shined His light
Showing me His holy way

I have found true peace
Happiness, Joy and Love
It's only temporary in the world
But abundant from above

Maybe you can be next
Just put your will down
Begin to follow Jesus
And his love will be found

I Left The World Behind

I left the world behind
And God is not far away
I can hear Him when He speak
And understand the things He say

He told me to live Holy
And leave the world behind
He said that I should be an example
And a light for those who are blind

I have left the world behind me
Please understand
I don't claim to be better than any one
It's just that someone needs to take a stand

To leave the world behind
Means to step away from the crowd
Separate yourself to be used by God
And you will surely make Him proud

Larry Williams

I'm Going On

I'm going on
After the storm and rain
What has happened
I can not change

I'm moving with God
In the name of love
Praying for direction
From Heaven above

My heart was heavy
But I learned to forgive
I became a light
And now I can live

I'm Just A Child

I'm just a child
And I can really get out of control
I need someone to help me
And give me a hand that I can hold

I want to prosper in life
Be someone who has a good name
I need the discipline that God says
Will keep my parents from shame

I hear that Satan has been deceiving
And really hurting my little friends
Well I'm going to take a stand
I would like to see this end

I would rather have a little spanking now
Than a beating when I'm old
This is what the word of God says
Will help save my soul

In My Will Lord

Lord I'm in my will
And see no way out
I really don't understand
Why the saints jump and shout

Will you share with me
What they've been told
Lord I need some faith
My will is getting old

My days are like nights
And my nights are so long
I know in my heart
That my will is wrong

Lord I'm ready
To turn my will in
I'm going back to church
And I will live free from sin

It's Getting Late

It's getting late
And the hour is near
The Lord is going to call
And we all will have to leave here
Death is sure to come
And then Heaven or Hell awaits
We need to live a holy and righteous life now
Before it's too late
Lord, Lord we cry
In our time of need
As soon as the need is met
We sow another bad seed
Saying Lord please have mercy on me
He says your gilt remains because you claim you can see
God gives a choice
As to whom you can serve
If you choose Satan
Then you have ignored His word
Refusing Christ is one's greatest mistake
But you have another chance
Don't wait to late
The church today is as a play ground
With ungodly leadership
You are guaranteed to stay down
But don't just lay down
You could be that Daniel of today
And just slay the lion
That gets in your way

Jesus Built The Church

Jesus built the church
The one that is true
The one He's coming back for
When the time is due

This church is His people
Those who live as they should
According to His purpose
Just the way He would

A church is good to have
For the assembling of the saints
But be assured of God's presence
Not just boards bricks and planks

Judge Me Not

Judge me not
Is the plea of the world
Tell all' of God's Gospel
Every man, woman, boy and girl

No I'm not a judge
I'm just a saint you see
God told me to notice
The fruit of every tree

Know who you are
And do not be deceived
One thing is for certain
This world you will leave

So judge me not
The final day is near
Will you be found in the Lord
Or live that day in fear

Larry Williams

Left To Yourself

Left to yourself
You're as dead man's bones
Satan will take possession
Your chance at Heaven will be gone

When you're left to yourself
It's impossible to see
When you're left to yourself
You're exactly where Satan wants you to be

Don't be left to yourself
Not for one more day
Choose God and live
There is no better way

Let Us Reason Together

Let us reason together
We are Christians, who are made to love
Let us find peace
Which is a gift that comes from above

Reason with me
Let's understand right from wrong
One brings peace the other brings chaos
Let's leave chaos alone

Let us reason together
Take no one for granted, that is no good
Give out what you expect in return
You already know that you should

Reasoning is of God
Satan's hand is not involved
He's the author of confusion
So reason' and get the problem solved

Living For God

Living for God
It comes with a price
You're at spiritual warfare
For the rest of your life

Someone close to you
May walk out the door
But they're not the first to be deceived
Satan has done this before

He fights us with our love ones
He hits from every side
But keep showing love
Don't be over taken with pride

For the battle is spiritual
And it will be hard
Stay set in your faith
And keep living for the Lord

Living Testimony

Do you finally get it
Do you now understand
The pain was for your good
God just had to use a man

If we have no problems
How will we grow
There is nothing we could tell
Because we wouldn't know

Be a living testimony
And explain your past
Tell how your troubles
Gave you strength that will last

What doesn't kill you
Will only make you grow
Your strength will be great
Christ in you will start to show

Love

There's no other answer
Nothing else to say
God is love
And He's the only way

Love is spiritual
True and bright
Without God in it
It's as dark as night

Get to know God
And you'll know love
It always shines
And it comes from above

Love Your Neighbor As Yourself

If I could move a mountain
People would scream and shout my name
But if I didn't love my neighbor
It wouldn't mean a thing

God's love is the missing ingredient
In the body of the church
If the love of God is missing
How on earth can the church work

We all have responsibilities as saints
To let our light shine before all men
Especially in the house of the Lord
Where one comes to leave their burdens and sins

You will be despised and rejected by some
But don't worry it's okay
Satan will forever do his part
Just don't let him use you that way

If you have the love of God in you
You don't have to tell a soul
Your light is bright and shining
Every one simply knows

Misery Loves Company

Don't let darkness
Over shadow your light
For misery loves company
And it's looking for a fight

Misery is a spirit
One that is sad and depressed
Out to steal your joy
And make your life a mess

Pray for the miserable
For they are in a dark place
Pray that peace will take over
And they will start to seek God's face

My Beautiful Wife

I thank God
For my beautiful wife
Next to Him
She's first in my life

Whenever I'm down
She knows just what to do
I'm so thankful God
That her spirit is of you

What did I do
To deserve such a gift
I don't know
But praise I lift

So thank you God
For sending me someone true
She and I together
Have your work to do

My Own Worst Enemy

One can be his or her own worst enemy
By the choices that they make
A bad tree will not produce good fruit
Let a righteous path be the one that you take

Someone is always pointing a finger at Satan
Saying he did it, it's all his fault
Now they're sorry for all that they've done wrong
But are really sorry that they got caught

Have I been my own worst enemy
Was I holding on to the Devil and He was trying to get away
Being your own worst enemy has devastating consequences
And it's a hell of a price to pay

My Saved Husband

I thank God
For a husband like you
Your heart is pure
And you're God fearing too

You are truly handsome
And I mean from inside out
When we first talked
I wanted to shout

The peace of God
Rest upon your soul
It's easy to tell
Because your spirit shines like gold

God thank you
And I promise I will serve
I will be the wife you said I should be
According to your word

Peace

Peace needs to be sought by all
For without it, we are sure to fall
Satan is busy seeking whom he may devour
But don't let him steal your peace
In this final hour
Love is the ingredient that cast out fear
But we still need peace
To keep our love ones near
If peace is afar nowhere to be found
There has to be an evil spirit
That's keeping you bound
There is power in peace
Power that no demon understands
Power that gives you a relationship
With all of God's commands
Follow after peace
Until your last day
When you notice that it's missing
You simply have to pray

Preacher

Preacher, preach the uncompromising word
Let the crowds be astonished
At the Doctrine
That they've heard

Stay prayed up
And keep your eye on the Lord
Satan's out to get you
So make his Job hard

You're God's chosen one
So let your light shine
You have to be the example
And holy all the time

Questioned by God

God: why did you ignore me until you needed my help
Soul: I'm a very busy person and most things I could do myself
God: why did you defile your temple, I desired it to be clean
Soul: well God I like to get high, have sex, over eat, smoke and drink,
that was just my thing
God: Did you not know that I am jealous and I must be first in line
Soul: my flesh requires lots of attention, I assumed you didn't mind
God: why did you lie so much, did truth bring you fear
Soul: no I liked telling lies and being told what I like to hear
God: why didn't you show all people love, that was one of my greatest
commands
Soul: well they just weren't on my level and some of them I couldn't stand
God: what about the people you hurt, did you go back and make
amends
Soul: no I figured they would be okay, I could always get new friends
God: why did you judge your neighbor, and you were once in that fight
Soul: well they should have known better, and it just wasn't right
God: why did you go to a false church, and you knew that I wasn't there
Soul: I liked to see the preacher perform and the choir was beyond
compare
God: was I not enough, my son died for your sins
Soul: yes Lord I know, and I'm ready to make amends
God: I never knew you, it's time for us to depart
Aren't you glad that this is just a warning and you have a chance for a
brand new start

Religion

Religion is the tool
That has divided the church
Have you checked yours lately
Are you sure that it works

Jesus is the way
The truth and the life
And when he comes back
We all need to have it right

There is power in his name
And believe me it's real
I pray that your religion recognizes The Father's Son
I've seen the demons run and the people healed

Rumors

Entertaining rumors
That you don't know to be true
Is truly entertaining
Until those rumors are about you

Satan Says

Nothing unrighteous moves me
I sit around these churches week after week
The power of God is missing
I can tell when they pray and they speak
I'm an evil spirit
It takes righteousness to outdo me
Most of you won't live like this
And I don't have to flee
Most churches today
Only have a form of Godliness
It's not the real thing
I love going to these places
I like to buck, shout and scream
The choir sounds really good
That was my job and I did it well
I hope none of them are saved
We can sing and live together in hell
Oh yeah' the apple of my eye
A hypocriting preacher, what a dream
Causing souls to stay unsaved and lost
That's the reason why I sing
What joy comes to my heart
When I see you, using my schemes
Fighting cussin and fussin
Acting wicked and being mean
Just wanted you to know that I'm here
And if you need me don't bother to call
I'll be the one back stabbing, cutting your throat
And waiting for you to fall

Satan says (pt. 2)

I just couldn't stop there
I need to make this as clear as a bell
I'm so thankful to all those parents
Who have helped guarantee their child's soul to Hell

There are lots of people who don't truly know God
I love it, it makes my day
They think you can just put these children in time out
But the rod of correction is the only way

You see the Holy Spirit has not been welcomed into peoples' homes
So that's where me and my boys go to stay
Godless living draws me and my folk near
And you all wonder why these kids are gay

My job has gotten a lot easier
Leaders have taken a stand
They pray and shout but they are helping me out
If they are living with blood stained hands

A big shout out to all the hypocrites
Who are leading in the church
And most of all, to those who are governing the discipline of a child
Please keep up the good work

Smoking

Smoking is not natural
It causes disease to the heart
Your temple is meant to be Holy
Sanctified and set apart

Satan has a claim on your life
One that you can't see
He's waiting to devour
And claim his victory

Call him a liar
And let the habit go
Sanctify your temple
And watch your spirit grow

Larry Williams

Something Powerful Is Going To Happen

Something powerful is going to happen
There are many who don't believe
The day is fast approaching
When all will fall to their knees

A swift move of God is eminent
Just you wait and see
Atheist will begin to shout out
Lord I now believe

A massive move of God is coming
We've done it our way too long
Some of us are so complacent
We don't feel that we are wrong

Souls are at hand
We won't turn from our wicked ways
Something powerful is going to happen
It could be years, months or days

God is God all alone
Choose him now or continue to wait
Something powerful is going to happen
Let's pray you don't wait too late

The Back Slidden Preacher Confesses

The back slidden preacher confesses
He says yes I've been born again but I know you can't tell
I envy evil doers and things that are not like God
And my sin sick soul is starting to smell
How far will this go
I'm doing things I never dreamed
Have I been turned over to a reprobate mind
This is exactly how it seems
My love ones see me falling
And they reach out because they want to help
But my rejection is strong
I tell them to just save their self
Seems that I have lots of friends now
Who wants to party all the time
Watching me fall into a devils Hell
And praying that I will stay blind
The people who really love me
Tell me about the things that I should fear
The demons assigned to bring and keep me down
Tell me only that which sounds good to my ear

The Difference

Away with false religion
And the traditions and doctrines with in
The saints of God are hungry
And fed up with just following men

Yes there is a difference
In those that God chose and anointed
And then there are those who just showed up
And somehow got appointed

It takes the anointing of God to break strong holds
And to cast down sin
A pure heart and the simple truth
Is where the difference begins

The Gay Spirit

Where does the gay spirit come from
It comes from Satan and it's a sin
Everybody is born with some kind of affliction
But we all have to be born again

A gay spirit is one that is very strong
It grabs a hold to you and doesn't want to let go
This spirit is not of God in any fashion
It's the anti-Christ and you need to know

It takes the power of God to dismiss this spirit
To send this demon on his way
He is trying to kill you, he wants to take you out
And he is against any and every thing that God has to say

God says to be fruitful and multiply
But a child, two gay people can not create
Please open your eyes to Satan's deception and lies
I pray you don't wait too late

Larry Williams

The Great Deceiver

The great deceiver
Has reeled many souls in
They think they are okay
Even in their sin

He says just pay your tithes
And things will be well
Be sure and give a good offering
And many stories I will tell

We will sing beautiful songs
And have a good time
Any message that might offend you
I will leave behind

Let's just get together
And enjoy the show
We don't' need to talk about sin
That message has got to go

So stay where you are
Things are really great
I've been able to deceive you
You've been eating from my plate

The Light on the Hill

I am the light on the hill
I am the salt of the Earth
This was predestined in me
From the day of my birth

I have to shine
Before all men
I can't be caught up
And mixed into Sin

God is my source my shield
And my rock
He has given me favor
And I must not stop

The Money Line

The money line is moving
The preacher said that Jesus is coming back soon
And we need to raise at least ten thousand
Before anyone leaves this room

One man was on his way out the door
The usher said where are you going
He said I gave all that I have to give
I don't have any more money for sowing

He said he gave his tithe and offering
But they just kept asking for more
He said that God wasn't convicting him to give
So what is this really for

He said that he thought the church was a hospital for sinners
And he was as spiritually sick as he could be
He said the spirit of God told him to keep his money
Cause salvation is absolutely free

The Wise Discipline their Children

Discipline is needed
In a child's life
They're no other options
Only division and strife

Punishment that hurts
Will chase evil from his heart
This is God's will
Stand up and do your part

Your child is crying out
That discipline is his need
It's time for you to rule
Don't let Satan sow the seed

If there is no discipline
Where will it all end
This spirit is not of God
And its name is simply SIN

Larry Williams

Through My Trials

Through my trials
I tossed and I turned
I opened my Bible
And the word I learned

I placed it in my heart
And I was not the same
God's spirit moved in
And took the heat from the flame

My trials built me up
From when I was torn down
My faith is now in God
And trials don't have me bound

A trial is just a test
A measure of your faith
Turn it over to God
And you have won the race

To Us

Let's have a celebration
And give God his praise and glory
He allowed us to be here
In health to share our story

We stayed together in hard times
It's easy to just give up
God is the rock that we built on
It wasn't convenience or luck

Love kept us here
Not fear of being alone
So to us my love let's celebrate
And thank God our house is a home

Tomorrow

Tomorrow is the day
That the world depends on
Tomorrow may be the day
That the world is gone

Don't be deceived
Thinking that there's time left
Seal your salvation
Before your date with death

Don't take a chance
On dying in sin
Satan is eagerly waiting
For your soul to come in

Tomorrow is a mystery
And no one knows
But it's surely your choice
Where your soul goes

Walking With the Lord

This walk I'm walking
Needs to be looked at right
For I'm walking with the Lord
And it comes with a fight

Jesus was talked about
And lied on too
If you truly walk with him
Your persecution is due

Keep peace in your heart
When lies start to flow
When the ones close walk away
Just pray and let them go

This walk I'm walking
Comes with a made-up mind
It means to live for God
And leave this world behind

Larry Williams

What a Friend

It's said that friends are hard to find
And I find that to be true
But I thank God this day
For blessing me with you
You were there when I was in need
No one else seemed to care
You didn't have much to give
But you found a way to share
Blessed am I to have you
You are truly a faithful friend
Love, peace and blessings
We are friends to the end

Whatever it takes

Whatever it takes
Lord I'm willing to do
You gave your life for me
And I'm giving mine to you

What will it profit a man
To gain the world
But die and loose his soul
No treasure is worth salvation
Not silver or gold

So whatever it takes
Lord my life I give
I'll be that example
Of how your people should live

What if

What if God operated like man
And only thought of us one day of the week
He may forget to give us vision
Or a voice so that we can speak

What if you couldn't talk to him
When you pleaded your case, he only got mad
Said you complain too much
Things are really not that bad

What if he was lazy
Or just didn't have time
What if he had better things to do
And assumed we didn't mind

What if God said it's time
The world ends today
Do you think that you are ready
Do you think you'll be okay

What will it take

What will it take
For your light to come on
If you don't choose soon
Your chance maybe gone

How could you miss God
You have been deceived
Satan robs you of life
God gives you air to breath

What will it take
To lose someone close
God is the father
He should mean the most

So what will it take
Let's hope not your soul
God requires your praise
Take heed you've been told

When God Is In the Room

It was early one Sunday morning
And Jesus was on my mind
I went out to the house of the Lord
I knew that there was something that I had to find

As soon as I walked through the door
It consumed me, I didn't have to wait
The spirit of God was there
And nothing about it was fake

I never had a preacher to tell me that I could make it
And that I didn't have to tip and dip in sin
He said that if I didn't live my life Holy, I was going to Hell
And he wasn't in town to make friends

When God is in the room
There is a super spiritual flow
Demons tremble and fall to their knees
They have to loose you and let you go

When You Get Caught

Who's praying for me
Now that I've been exposed
I guess God was watching the whole time
And now everybody knows

I was doing exactly what I like
It really felt good to my flesh
God obviously had a problem with me
Because He allowed me to be exposed in my mess

I told the people that I had fallen
You know, we fall but get back up
But actually I laid down and was quiet comfortable in my sin
But then I had bad luck

Somebody told on me
I didn't mean for them to tell it, it wasn't my fault
I guess all good things must come to an end
Especially when you get caught

Where Is The Love

Where is the love
That one expects, when they walk into God's church
Has the love of God died?
This is what a sinner will think if they don't see it at work

Imagine walking into God's house
And starring into faces made of stone
It turns sinners even Christians away
Makes them want to leave God's house alone

So where is the love
God says love your neighbor as yourself
Do you think your neighbor feels loved
If you didn't say hi before they left

The word Christian means Christ like
And that's how we are supposed to be
Anyone who is truly Christ like
Wouldn't have a problem speaking to me

So where is the love
Remember to always let your light shine
The hardest part of being a Christian is easy
You simply have to be kind

Why Me God

Why me God
Why not you
Instead of my way
You did what you wanted to

Was I an option
Was I even a choice
Did you not understand
Could you not hear my voice

You chose the path
And you chose to go
I said in my word
That you will reap what you sow

So change your mind
And begin to pray
Put me first
And let me be the way

You May Be Just Religious

You may be just religious
If you have a form of Godliness but deny the power within
You may be just religious
If you say you love God and your life is stilled filled with sin

You may be just religious
If you go to church to show off what you have on
You may be just religious
If there is never any church in the place that you call home

You may be just religious
If you think God didn't call a woman to preach
You may be just religious
If you don't know His voice when He speaks

Religion is man made
And by its self it is dead
There has to be a connection to Jesus and Holy living
This is what God said

Your Life

Your life in this world
Is swiftly passing away
God made sacrifices
What price will you have to pay

Don't go on thinking
That you're so great
That you can live without God
And his air you can take

You're being deceived
By the evil one himself
He will drain your soul
Until there's nothing left

This fleshly world
Is simply a part of your test
God just wants to know
Where to lay your soul to rest

Notes

Notes

Notes

Notes

Notes

LaVergne, TN USA
06 April 2011
223204LV00002B/55/P